Eight
Strands
of
Gold

Earl Gilbert

Life Chronicles Publishing
Give your life a voice!

ISBN: 978-1-958242-07-0

Editor: Crystal Hines

Life Chronicles Publishing Copyright © 2023

lifechroniclespublishing.com

Contents

Eight Strands of Gold

Introduction

It was a very pleasant warm spring afternoon, and I was sitting on my patio bench. I was in a relaxed state of mind, spirit, soul, and body. While gazing into the outer atmosphere of my thoughts without questioning where or why, the following trilogy was messaged to me: "What is the most powerful tool given to Humanity? "What is the most Precious Commodity given to Humanity?" And, "What is the Thread which Binds them?"

As I pondered, somewhat perplexed yet with exhilarating anticipation—waiting for an epiphany— these messages were gifted to me:

The Mind is the most powerful tool for everything; they include our thoughts, imaginations, desires, fantasies, and most importantly, our beliefs. Secondly, an essential commodity is time. Because without it, there would be no sense of order—minutes turn to hours, which turn into days, which lead to weeks and weeks to months, months to years, as well as seasons, and what is vital is what takes place between birth and death. The final answer to this trilogy followed this, "How We Use Them," is the thread that binds! How do we use our minds and the time gifted to us from birth to death as a window filled with life situations, circumstances, and experiences that allow us ample opportunities to realize the most important factor—what is my "LIFE PURPOSE"?

Long before life as we know it, the indigenous peoples learned the most important Law of all, "The Law of Order for the Preservation Of Life." In the Genesis creation story, everything is based on these two factors, order and time; meaning again, as told in scripture, the entire cosmos was created in six days, beginning with light.

There I was, still sitting on the patio bench and pondering all this profound information, realizing how easy it is for many never to find their true purpose. Many in my generation were born in two-parent households, with primary influencers being the father (male figure) and mother (female figure)—they imposed thoughts and feelings about specific social issues and beliefs regarding religion and God. Followed by other influencers such as siblings, grandparents, aunts/uncles, school teachers, social media, and the most underrated detrimental influencer was slavery, meaning its ability to damage a person's psyche for multiple generations.

So, after contemplating these various trains of thought, I was compelled to test the waters of other perspectives regarding this trilogy of questions. With no further reason to continue sitting on the patio bench, I went into the house with no one better for me than my wife. At the time, she was preparing brunch, an egg four-cheese omelet with mushrooms, cilantro, jalapeno, bell peppers, homemade biscuits, and sausage. As she continued to prepare the meal, she lent me an ear, and so the questioning began, "What is the most powerful tool given to humanity?" followed by "What is the most precious commodity?" and lastly, "What is the thread which Binds them?" She said,

"Hmm, let me think about these questions for a while," so I went into the living room, turned on the television, and watched some golf. Shortly after she finished cooking, she came and said, "Those are some very deep questions," but here are my answers; I believe that the most powerful tool given to us is our mind because this is where we receive knowledge from the most precious commodity, God, who is our creator. I feel as though love is what binds them together."

She then asked, "How did I do?" I told her there are no right or wrong answers, and the objective is to visit our social consciousness and its varying perspectives. Right, and Wrong are two major influences imposed upon us from the day we are born by ourselves and others. I've come to learn that this life experience is made up of a continuous compilation of life situations that call for us to make choices. Life circumstances follow these choices and the results or consequences of those choices. But what about God? What happens when we say there is no God? Does believing this way result in the outcome of our existence? I think that there is a being that some call God. I believe in

"PTOLEION"—FATHER GOD, THE GIFTER OF LOVE, AND THE ESSENCE OF LIFE! As well as Ancestral Beings who live in another realm and a different state. Remember, this is my perspective; I do not wish to impose this on anyone. Let's call it a Love share moment from the author to the reader.

So, after this new train of thought, it was time to test the waters of other perspectives with this trilogy of questions. The next person I chose to love-share this trilogy of questions with was my daughter, the oldest of our three children. If you, the reader, don't mind, I won't repeat, but I would like to love-share with you her answers. Again, much like her mom and everyone else I asked, she would need a little time to listen, think, hear, and then share. So I gifted her the time, and here's what she shared, "God is the most powerful tool, wisdom is the most precious commodity, and peace is what binds them." After sharing, she asked, "How did I do?" And like I told her mom, I told her there are no right or wrong answers but various perspectives.

Let me love-share with you again my views on this trilogy. To me, the mind is the most powerful tool given to humanity; time is the most precious commodity, and how we use them is what binds them. So as you continue to read this metaphor of my playwright, please take the time to listen, think and hear from your mind, spirit, soul, and body.

Over the next few months, I was led to ask as many people who would lend me their ear this trilogy of questions to get a glimpse of the social consciousness from a few perspectives. After reading and re-reading the various views shared with me, it was clear that this trilogy would be the foreshadow of Eight Strands of Gold. The purpose of Eight Strands of Gold is to challenge all who read it to listen, think, and hear from the apex of their mind, spirit, soul, and body to understand that each life situation and life circumstance may bring about a more pleasant and peaceful love-sharing Life Experience.

My message to the reader is that All have been Gifted the Gift of Life, some the Gift to Produce, and if not Gifted to Produce, still Gifted to Provide and Protect. As seen in the Law of Order for the Preservation of Life, All have been Gifted the Right to

Live a Pleasant and peaceful love sharing LIFE by Ptoleion Our Father God, who is Love—The essence of Life!

Eight Strands of Gold

Love

Love is, loving someone unconditionally, faithfully, wisely and willingly.

Love is wise when practiced fairly.

Love is wise when practiced justly.

Love is wise when practiced faithfully.

Love is wise when practiced willingly.

Love is wise when practiced wisely.

Love is wise when practiced lovingly.

Love is wise when practiced open.

Love is wise when practiced sharingly.

Love is lovingly lovely when practiced justly and respectfully.

Love is lovingly just when practiced fairly and dependently.

Love is justifiably faithful when practiced openly and faithfully.

Love is faithfully fair when practiced pleasantly and peacefully.

Love is prosperously pleasant when practiced responsibly and tactful.

Love is promotingly prosperous when practiced silently and carefully.

Love is patiently patient when practiced gently and kindly.

Love is pleasurably pleasurable when practiced friendly and unconditionally.

Love is eternally bliss when practiced faithfully and one day at a time.

Love is heartful giving when practiced willfully and honestly.

Love is especially warm when practiced lovingly and caringly.

Love is playful fun when practiced joyously and freely.

Love is inner strength when practiced watchfully and prayerfully.

Love is pleasant peace when practiced devoted and sincere.

Love is persistently alive when practiced consistently with drive.

Love is All we need when practiced with God at the lead.

Love is always a willing act of kindness when practiced peacefully.

Love is always a willing act of pleasantness when practiced pleasant.

Love is always a willing act of blissfulness when practiced patiently.

Love is always a willing act of being when practiced willingly.

Love is always a willing act of prayerfulness when practiced prayerfully.

Love is always a willing act of justice when practiced restlessly.

Love is always a willing act of patience when practiced justly.

Love is always a willing act of peace when practiced wisely.

Life
Experience

I attended school at Holland House while living in Wichita Falls, Texas. I was introduced to another student who had just lost his father and younger sister while doing a standard weekend family love-share moment. His father was an officer and pilot at Shepard Air Force Base, and periodically he would take his children out for practice flights. Unfortunately, there was a malfunction in the aircraft, which led to

his fathers' and sisters' demise, as he stood and watched. Because of this unexpected tragic incident, he could no longer cope with attending classes at any of the other three high schools; he lost all ambition and desire to willingly participate in any outside activities, choosing instead to be a loner—accepting whatever fate brought his way.

All of this was shared with me by the janitor, who also was the pastor of a Methodist church. This pastor pulled me aside and asked me to share with this young man what I had shared with him about the accident my family was in some five years ago. The pastor also mentioned how this other student no longer believed in God and blamed him for losing his father and sister. So, I willingly approached this student and pleasantly introduced myself, and he peacefully returned the gesture. Now that the ice had been broken, I carefully and prayerfully began to share with him first what the pastor and I had discussed so that he would know. Then how God delivered me and my family from an accident that had, over time, claimed at least one hundred lives. While riding in a 1967 valiant, all eight of us went over a cliff at a thirty to sixty-foot drop and landed on a boulder. We came out alive; however, the other ninety-nine people who traveled that road did not. We were delivered from the gully of death by the hand and love of God. So, after sharing this with him, I paused and said, "I understand how much the loss of your father and sister hurts because there was another family member who was in college, and she thought that she had lost all of us until my mom told my dad to call the college and let her know that yes we were all alright and in recovery. I suffered a fractured skull and was given a fifty percent chance to live, and even if I made it through surgery, I would most likely be bedridden for the rest of my life. But look at us; we are here for a reason." He quietly listened periodically, saying, "Why, I was supposed to go on the first ride; it should have been me!" With a very gentile response, "I said yes, but evidently God has a greater life purpose for you, so trust God and know that he loves and cares for you. After what I call a love-share moment, he asked me what church I attended, and I told him. The following Sunday, guess who was there?

Wisdom

**Wisdom is Faithfully, Justly practicing
Fairness on behalf of All.**

Wisdom cannot be used to Justify a pleasant pleasurable unfair act. Lynching

Wisdom can be used to peacefully please a prominent act of pleasure.

Wisdom can be used to create a very loving act of wellness.

Wisdom is a strand of gold sent from God for order and the preservation of life.

Wisdom is to be used wisely.

Wisdom sets apart acts of selfish-servitude and acts of serving God.

Wisdom is not for the use of control over others but to help others find purpose.

Wisdom is a very prominent gift from God for the well-being of All.

Wisdom, when practiced fairly and pleasantly, brings about peace and pleasure.

Wisdom, when practiced wisely and peacefully, brings about love and restoration.

Wisdom, when practiced justly and fairly brings about a pleasant bliss.

Wisdom when practiced impartial brings about pleasant patience.

Wisdom when practiced prayerfully and faithfully brings about a pleasurable result.

Wisdom, when practiced steadfastly and uncompromisingly, brings about unmeasurable results of justice.

Wisdom when practiced constitutionally correct brings about a United Nation.

Wisdom when practiced Justly, fairly in the courts for the well-being of All can bring about a platform to resolve social discord.

Wisdom is wonderfully just when practiced peacefully.

Wisdom is wisely fair when practiced pleasantly.

Wisdom is faithfully pleasant when practiced uncompromisingly.

Wisdom is blissfully patient when practiced lovingly.

Wisdom is peacefully wise when practiced patiently.

Wisdom is graciously uncompromising when practiced fairly.

Wisdom is pleasurably pleasant when practiced passionately.

Wisdom is justifiably just when practiced wisely.

Life
Experience

It was the summer of 1972; I was twelve, and the family was living with Grandmother Juanita. One day after summer school, my best friend asked if I was going to play minor baseball because a man who lived down the street from him was putting a team together of boys from the neighborhood. Dennis told me if I were interested, he would come and get me, and we could go to the park where the tryouts would occur. I said, "ok." So, I went home and got permission from my parents. After that, I went and sat on the front porch and waited for Dennis. When he arrived, he told me that the tryouts were at the park on 42nd and park avenue. Upon arrival, I saw many classmates sitting on the bleachers. So, Dennis and I went to the bleachers, sat near the others, and waited for the coach to arrive.

When the coach arrived, he pulled bags with baseballs, gloves, and bats out of his car. He told us to pick a position that we felt you could play. I chose outfield mainly because my favorite player then was

Willie Mays, one of the greatest outfielders ever to play the game. Looking around, I noticed that Jackie chose the position of pitcher, Dennis shortstop, and Arthur catcher. After a few pitches, the coach approached the mound and asked Jackie if he had ever played baseball; Jackie said no, then he asked if anyone knew how to pitch. Jackie's brother said I can, and so the switch was made. Our first practice was bunted to infielders and popups to outfielders; this took place for about two hours, and it was clear that Dennis was the best player. The rest of us were rough edges that needed work. The coach had us try playing different positions for the next two weeks. After two weeks of position and batting practice, the coach announced who made the team, and the roster was set. I played centerfield, Arthur was a catcher, and Dennis was recruited by the coach from another league of older boys.

The season included seven six-inning games with a playoff between the top two teams. Our first game was against, The Sons of the Kansas City Athletics, and they crushed us. I don't even think we scored a run, but the lesson to be learned was how disciplined they were at each position; these were words of wisdom from our coach. Throughout the next week, as we prepared for our next game, the coach asked Jim to be his assistant, and Jim accepted the offer. Jim would spend time with us, mainly hitting ground balls to infielders and popups to outfielders and showing us how to hold the bat and choose the correct bat for our swing. Unfortunately, some of the guys still fell short of taking it seriously, and their lack of discipline showed in game two again. Yes, we lost, but we scored a run. Before our next practice, Jim said, "I have some sad news, coach's mother passed away, and he had to leave and doesn't know when he will be back, but before he left, he talked to Pappa Bell and asked him if he could take over until he returned." Pappa Bell said, "Yes." The first thing I remember Pappa Bell doing was taking us to another park to practice. At the end of our first practice with Pappa Bell, he asked me if I was interested in pitching, and I said, "Sure, why not." He said, "Good, wait here; let me talk to the rest of the team about the schedule for our next practice." Pappa Bell then loaded up his van and took my brother and me out to Swope Park, a nice quiet, cool spot well-shaded where we would throw balls back and forth to each other for about forty minutes, after which he said, "Come over to my house tomorrow after summer school, I have something set up for you that will help you learn the fundamentals of pitching."

So, the next day after summer school, I went home first and asked my parents if I could go over to Coach Bell's house to practice pitching, and they both said, "Ok, see you when you get back." I lived five minutes from Coach Bell, and when I arrived, my brother was already there in the backyard with Pappa Bell waiting. There were three marked spots in the yard. Coach Bell had each of us pick one and then look forward to the three tires hanging under three windows; Coach Bell then explained that our job was to throw the ball into the center of our designated tire without breaking the window. We looked at each other with fear and asked how we were supposed to do that. Coach Bell said, "Don't worry if you break a window; I will cover the cost." So, slowly and carefully, we all began to toss balls at the tires; Pappa Bell told us to stop, listen, and see the tire as a batter we were facing and figure out how to get the ball over the plate. After a few more throws, I finally got one through the center of my tire without breaking the window. After that, finding a release point and determining how much velocity and control was needed became much easier. My brother and the other guy broke a window, and neither found the center of their tires, so coach bell told them to stop and watch me throw a few balls. Was I able to throw all the balls into the center of the tire? No, but I was able to stay away from the window! Up to this point, Jackie's brother was the starting pitcher, but things were about to change.

The following day at practice, coach bell named me the starting pitcher going into game three; after losing the first two games, we were at the bottom of the standings. I was a little timid at the beginning of the game, but after the first three innings, I settled down and completed the game with a win. We were also able to win the next game, only to find out that Pappa Bell would be taking a vacation and would be gone for the next two weeks. I wondered who would be our coach while Pappa Bell was gone. I didn't know that Coach Bell and my dad had already met and agreed on my dad coaching the team for the next two games. I felt proud that the coach felt confident having my dad take over until he returned.

Game five became the pivotal point of our season, we were in a three-way tie for second place, and we would be playing the team that just beat the team in first place. With a win, we would move to second place. While standing on the mound throwing some warm-up pitches, I noticed how some of the players on the other team were looking and laughing at me as if to say they were going to clobber me. Well, it was not so easy, and we pulled off a win! The score was seven to five with bases loaded in the bottom of the sixth, with a strikeout. I didn't have my best stuff, and my brother was out with a cold, but we survived a scare. Game six was the one that would either clinch us a spot in the playoffs or move us back into a tie with two other teams, and it just so happens it was against the Kansas City Athletics.

There are times when we experience a life situation that gives birth to a moment that we will remember throughout our lives; that moment was about to take place. While on the mound throwing practice pitches, I could feel an air of overconfidence regarding the opposing team, yet I was very relaxed and pleasantly at peace as the game began. The first inning had no hits at all, only strikeouts. During the second inning, I noticed how much bigger this batter seemed, and it intimidated me to the point that my first pitch to him was so wild that my dad called a time-out. As he approached the mound, I knew this wasn't going to be good, and my dad pleasantly said, "I understand why you threw that pitch, it's because he looks bigger, but he's just another twelve-year-old boy like you, so pitch to him like you've pitched to everyone else not to his size. That throw told him that you are afraid of him." My dad asked me if I was afraid of him, and I said, "No." Before my dad left, he said, "Remember he's just another twelve years older like you; go get him." I did and went on to pitch a no-hitter against the first-place team again.

Those words of wisdom from my dad helped me refocus and keep everything in proper perspective. In retrospect, I found wisdom in each coach's role, not only in helping me but in how each one dealt with this life situation which would positively impact others.

Our first coach experienced the loss of his mother, but he still took the time to ensure his team would be coached by someone he felt confident about. Pappa Bell (before going on vacation) also made sure that the team would stay focused until he returned. Lastly, my dad gave me some of the most valuable information at this point of my life that I am still very grateful for to this day—"just because he's bigger doesn't mean he's better; pitch to him as you have pitched to the others and whatever happens let happen."

Fairness

Fairness is when someone in authority looks at a life situation concerning many and concludes it with a Just Cause and Reason.

Fairness is an act of positive outcome for all who are just.

Fairness is an act of positive outcome for those who seek truth.

Fairness is an act of positive outcome for those who ask for righteousness.

Fairness is an act of positive outcome for those who deserve reprove.

Fairness is an act of positive outcome for those who pray for peace.

Fairness is an act of positive outcome when one is very patient.

Fairness is an act of positive outcome when one approaches an unpleasant life situation with unwavering faith.

Fairness is an act of positive outcome when one is led by God.

Fairness will always prevail against unjust acts of cruelty.

Fairness will always prevail against unjust acts of authority.

Fairness will always prevail against unjust acts of power.

Fairness will always prevail against unjust acts of rulership.

Fairness will always prevail against unjust acts of law.

Fairness will always prevail against unjust acts of civil rights.

Fairness will always prevail against unjust acts of social discrimination.

Fairness will always prevail against unjust acts of inhumane atrocities.

Fairness overrules all unjust earthly affairs.

Fairness overrules all unjust governing rules.

Fairness overrules all unjust superficial plots.

Fairness overrules all unjust governing parties.

Fairness overrules all unjust governing mandates.

Fairness overrules all unjust governing sectors.

Fairness overrules all unjust practices.

Fairness overrules all unjust acts of partiality.

Life
Experience

I faced a very trying life situation many years ago while working at a private Christian school. I was the director of a prominent childcare program that exceeded all expectations as an African American education facility from preschool to middle school.

It was a regular day (or so it seemed); the energy was very upbeat and positive, as usual. Staff members and parents greeted one another with smiles, hugs, and short conversations as they went to their designations. The preschool was still celebrating the two million dollars contributed to the program by a well-known family once affiliated with the NBA and a private investor, which took place a few days before this incident.

After breakfast and when all of the preschool children were in their portables, I was approached by a parent asking if we could meet; I said yes, let's go to my office. After sitting down, she shared an unexpected and startling concern regarding one of my best preschool childcare providers. She said, "Yesterday when I was going to pick up my son, and I was stopped by another parent who told me that my son's childcare provider picked up my son and put him in the trashcan headfirst, and another boy was standing nearby crying." Then she shared with me that when she entered the room and asked the childcare provider if what the other parent told her was true, the provider said yes and then attempted to explain the reasoning behind her action. The concerned parent listened to the childcare provider but was reluctant to agree that this was the most appropriate and professional way to handle this situation. So she said she left without letting her know what steps she planned to take against her and the school if matters were not addressed seriously. So, instead of going to the director or any other figure of authority, I decided to come directly to your attention, Mr. Earl, because I believe, as does his father, that you will do the right thing. After this, she shared with me that she was an attorney and the boy's father, who was on his way, was a civil rights community activist. Shortly after, the father showed up, and I gathered my thoughts. I shared with them the plan of action I would take; first, I let them know that I was going to call my licensor and report this incident because, as a mandated reporter, I'm obligated to do so, and secondly, terminate this staff member because what she did calls for immediate termination, and lastly inform the director of the what and why of my actions. Both seemed pleased with this action plan, yet she stated very clearly that if this staff member is in the classroom tomorrow, a lawsuit will be filed, and every news channel will be contacted and informed about this act of negligence.

You see, the staff member that I had to release was the adopted daughter of the school director; on top of that, most of the staff grew up together attending the same schools as well as churches, and I was the new kid, so to say, on the block! Yet even then, I knew that when practiced wisely, fairness would bring about a pleasant and peaceful resolve.

After our meeting, I sat and prayed that God would gift me with his guidance and counsel as I carried out my plan of action. First, I made the call to my licensor and explained to her the reason for the call. She then reminded me that as a mandated reporter, I am obligated to terminate this staff member immediately to protect myself and the school, and then she wished me good luck. I then quietly strolled through the corridors from the preschool village to the upper-grade classrooms reminiscing on all the great contributions this staff member had given to the preschool program and how unfortunate it was that it came down to this. It was a dark, sullen walk and moment for me. When I arrived at her classroom, I quietly opened the door and stepped in, and she immediately had the children say, "Good morning, Mr. Earl," after which I asked her to step out into the hallway with me.

At this point, no one, not even the director, knew what was taking place; quietly, with great compassion, I told her that as your director and being a mandated reporter based on what occurred in your classroom yesterday, I must let you go immediately. With teary eyes and without fuss, she said she understood and asked if she could get her personal belongings after school not to cause any disruption in the classroom. I hugged her and said, "Yes." As I escorted her off the school premises, I didn't know the parents were watching from a distance.

After the teacher was gone, I approached them, and they informed me that they knew this was a challenging moment and were grateful that I resolved the issue quickly. We all walked to the school's director's office. I told her secretary the reason for our visit, and she immediately announced us. After meeting with the director, all agreed with the actions taken. My director decided not to dispute the results because she deemed them fair.

Justice

**Justice is a tool for the use of
separating good from evil.**

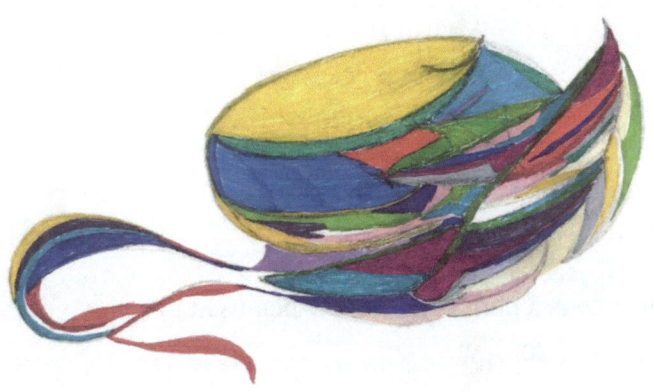

Justice is a perfect practice when used fairly for a righteous cause.

Justice is a perfect practice when used pleasantly for peace.

Justice is a perfect practice when used to defend against unjust brutality.

Justice is a perfect practice when used properly by those who hold the gavel.

Justice is a perfect practice when used to correct illegal activities in government.

Justice is a perfect practice when used for used for the wellbeing of all.

Justice is a perfect practice when used to bring order in social conflict.

Justice is a perfect practice when used with unwavering steadfast faith that the best decision has been reached.

Justice when practiced fairly will always prevail against unjust practices.

Justice when practiced justly will always prevail against acts of evil.

Justice when practiced wisely will always prevail against false accusations.

Justice when practiced pleasantly will always prevail against unpleasant acts of misconduct.

Justice, when practiced peacefully, will always prevail against those who misuse factual evidence.

Justice when practiced constitutionally will always prevail against unjust unconstitutional practices.

Justice when practiced fairly and justly will always prevail against racism, discrimination, apartheid, slavery, and most importantly white supremacy.

Justice when practiced Orderly for the Preservation of Life will always prevail for this is God's Law.

Life
Experience

It was the Open House for school and the night of the school play. My class was presenting; there were only two characters, and I was one. It was about a little boy growing up in the ghetto in a single-parent household and four other siblings.

The stage was set, and the play began...

It was a cold, dark winter night, and he was sitting on the steps in front of the apartments where he lived; the streetlights were very dim, making visibility difficult, and it was snowing. While sitting there, he wished he had a new pair of tennis shoes. As it got colder, he began to want them like right now, but he knew that his mother could not afford to buy him the new sneakers he saw daily in the store window on his way to school. Then he remembered that around this time, every night, the bus would come, and this lady would get off and slowly walk down the street all by herself. He didn't know that as the bus slowly approached the stop, that lady was gazing out the window and saw him, and that thing we call a woman's intuition kicked in. When she got off the bus, she held her purse very close and tight to her body. As the bus pulled away, she stood under the dim streetlight reaching into her coat pocket as if to be feeling for her house keys, and peeking out of the corner of her eyes, and she noticed that the boy was no longer sitting on the steps. He was sneakingly creeping up behind her; she then began to walk slowly down the sidewalk preparing for the inevitable purse snatch attempt. Hearing the pity padder of running feet, she stopped and braced herself for what would come. He grabbed for the purse, and she grabbed him by his arm; they wrestled for a while until she pinched one of his ears. She asked him, "Why are you trying to steal my purse? Before I got off the bus, I saw you sitting on those steps. Is that where you live?"

He said," Yes."

She said, "Come on, let's go talk to your parents."

The boy replied, "No, please don't tell my mama; I will do anything, but please don't tell what I did."

She asked him again, "Why did you try to take my purse?"

He said, "Because I need some new tennis shoes, and Mama can't afford to buy them."

The lady looked down at his feet and said to herself, yes, you do. She told the young man, "Come with me, and we can figure out a better way to get those new tennis shoes." After arriving at her apartment, she asked him, "Have you eaten dinner?"

He said, "No, I let my younger brothers and sisters eat, and if there's anything left, I eat and then clean up the dishes."

She looked at him and said, "Sit down at the table, and I'll be right back." After a few minutes, he could smell an aroma from the kitchen, making his stomach growl. She then came out of the kitchen with a plate of mashed potatoes with gravy, two pieces of chicken, cornbread, and some greens. After they finished eating, she took the plates to the kitchen, returned to the dining room table, and told him I've been thinking. If it's okay with your mama, you can come over to my place on Saturday and do some chores, and I will pay you, of course, and we will do this until you have enough to get those tennis shoes. She then went back into the kitchen and got a bag with food in it, and said come on, let's go talk to your mama.

You know the saying an idol mind is the devil's workshop? Poverty can allow wanting devils and wondering demons to lead someone to do very foolish things. This play reminded me that justice can be served in many different ways.

Eight Strands of Gold

Willingness

**Willingness is allowing God to Greatly
Gift you during turmoil!**

Willingness to serve will never lead one to submit to fear or doubt.

Willingness will always lead one to a Higher Plane of thought and action.

Willingness is a Great Gift from our father God.

Willingness will always lead one to the path of silent prayer that they may receive the gift of pleasant peace.

Willingness is like a great magnifying glass because it allows one to see how wonderful the gift of life from God is.

Willingness will never mislead one away from the fortune the Gift of Love that God has chosen for you.

Willingness is a Great Gift that teaches one how to listen think and hear with an open mind spirit soul and body in order to receive messages from God.

Willingness is a Great Gift that when unwrapped will give victory over the wishing imps wanting devils and wondering demons that were imposed in one's mind spirit and body by outside influencers.

Willingness is a plate with a meal of Love Peace and Pleasantness gifted to those who choose willingly to serve.

Willingness proves how Pleasantly Pleasant Life is meant to be.

Willingness will create a Life Experience far Greater than one could ever imagine.

Willingness will create in one a Mind of Creative Thinking a Spirit of Love Sharing a Soul to receive Godly messages and a Body to serve.

Willingness will always lead one to the Greatest Gift of All the Gift of Love the essence of Life!

Willingness is the beginning of one's rainbow with colors of love, peace, pleasantness wellness unveiling one's True-Life Purpose.

Willingness brings about moments to pleasantly peacefully love share with others throughout one's duration in this realm of life.

Willingness is like a seed that when planted spreads like wildfire producing fruits of love, peace, pleasantness and wellness everywhere.

Willingness will always help you to overcome your doubts and fears and replace them with the gift of inner strength and confidence.

Willingness is a great gift that equips one to succeed and never to fail.

Willingness is a Great gift which allows one to seek and recover that which was stolen.

Willingness is not for the foolish at heart but for those who chose to regain a sense of purity in mind spirit soul and body to listen think and hear the messages from God.

Willingness is a Great Gift from God who created all things for Order and the Preservation of Life.

Willingness is a Great Gift which leads one to their Life Purpose and like a warm cup of coffee it clears the mind, sooths the spirit, energizes the soul which allows the body to function.

Willingness is a Great Gift that opens one's mind spirit soul and body to receive the Greater Love Share Messages from God.

Willingness will never leave one in a state of confusion, but it will confuse those whose minds, spirit, soul and bodies are closed.

Life
Experience

Willingness is the first step in transforming one's Mind, spirit, soul, and body from all the negative karma imposed on them by others, knowingly and unknowingly. Throughout our lives, we tend to conform to the perspectives of many influencers, such as parents, teachers, clergy, social media, and extended family members. Which, in many cases, passed on to them from influencers of past generations. And so, when we become adults, we find ourselves left to sort out this karmic mess to find out who we really are and what life is really about. Remember, this is my perspective, and I feel that the Mind is the greatest tool gifted to all of humanity —this is where the thought of invention first takes place. When we look around us and see all of the significant structures created by man, such as the great Egyptian Pyramids, Statue of Liberty, Eiffel Tower, and different types of transportation, these objects were created by a group of superior people.

Willingness means to me, allowing God to greatly gift you during turmoil. Throughout our life experiences, we face many different life situations and circumstances. We are born into this realm of life dependent upon others to provide the nurturing love and care needed for our mental, physical, spiritual, and social growth and development. Willingly we receive and accept that which is being imposed in many cases without question. For example, why must I believe that there is a God who created heaven and earth and that the bible is His word of absolute truth? When you look at nature, have you ever asked yourself what law keeps animals from destroying one another? If I may love-share with you for a moment—when I look at nature, I see a rule of order for preserving life. The four elements, earth, wind, fire, and air, all preserve life.

My faith leads me to believe that there is one who created this place we call Earth and continues to create because it is infinite and that nothing dies but transforms from one state of being to another— transitioning to another realm of life. Willingness will lead one to fight for what is just, even if one must stand alone. It will cause one to go places and do things that will test their mental, physical, and spiritual resolve. Willingness will transform one from pity parties to silent prayer moments. Willingness is found throughout ancient books, such as Codex Sinaiticus, Leningrad Codex, Aleppo Codex, and Codex Alexandrinus. These books are available for a few to read, but many cannot because of the cost. But the book, free of charge and available for all to read pleasantly and peacefully, is misread daily. In ancient Kemet, it was called the Book of Life, and ancient indigenous peoples called it Nature.

Pleasantness

Pleasantness is a gift from our father God given
for us to enjoy Peace in Life.

Pleasantness is a gift for wellness in life.

Pleasantness is for all who willingly accept it and peacefully live it.

Pleasantness is a gift to those who willingly and peacefully live for the Glory of God.

Pleasantness will always keep one living in accordance with Gods law of order for the preservation of life.

Pleasantness is a gift of God's love and peace.

Pleasantness is a gift from God which gives peace to the mind spirit soul and body.

Pleasantness will always overshadow unpleasant acts and deeds.

Pleasantness will always create a better outcome when we face an adverse life situation.

Pleasantness, like a newborn child, brings an abundance of joy, happiness, peace and love.

Pleasantness, like the first ride on a bicycle, removes fear, worry and doubt replacing them with joy, happiness and inner confidence.

Pleasantness is like a young plant as it grows so to the fruits of joy, happiness and love.

Pleasantness like a well-aged wine gets better and better with the passing of time.

Pleasantness like a new ink pen used to write love shares with family and friends.

Pleasantness is like a new melody in song a masterpiece of music ping -ping-png- pong.

Pleasantness is like a warm smile it lifts you up to walk that extra mile.

Pleasantness is a gift and message from God, I will always lead you and be your guiding rod.

Pleasantness will always provide greater inner strength to fight for those whom one loves.

Pleasantness is a great gift given to those who choose to restlessly serve God.

Pleasantness helps relieve the mind spirit soul and body from stress.

Pleasantness like all strands of gold is infinite for it is a great gift from God.

Pleasantness will never abandon those whom God has chosen to lead others through darkness to light.

Pleasantness is like a beacon of light to guide one through the storms of life.

Pleasantness is like grandma's hot toddy it sooths the dis-eases of life.

Pleasantness is like a grain of salt it gives flavor to a bland menu life experience.

Life
Experience

It was Saturday morning, and everyone was getting ready for our trip to visit Grandpa Maddox. We needed to leave on time for two reasons. First, Daddy had to return to work, and second, to get to Grandpa's farm before the storm because of a tornado watch. It was about a three-hour drive from El Dorado, Kansas, to Muskogee, Oklahoma, and so Mama and Daddy loaded all seven of us into the little red station wagon, and off we went. As we crossed the border, the skies were filled with clouds, and it began to rain; Mama asked Daddy, "Earl do you think we should turn around and go back home? It doesn't look good."

Daddy said, "No, Joan, we can make it; we'll be there before the storm gets any worse."

So, Daddy continued driving to Grandpa's, and before you knew it, we were there. As we pulled up the driveway, I noticed a white man standing on the porch (at least, I thought he was white, only to find out later that he was Irish/Native American). As we got out of the car, the wind had picked up and was pretty strong; Grandpa and Daddy shook hands.

Mama said, "Hi, Daddy and hugged Grandpa.

He then said. "There's a tornado watch, expected to touch down soon. "Earl, are you going to stay or try to make it back?"

Daddy said, "I am going back, James."

They shook hands again, Daddy left, and we went into the storm cellar. While in the storm cellar, we could hear the strong winds as the tornado passed through Muskogee. Grandpa had a couple of lanterns and some blankets and, most importantly, food and water, oh yeah, and a designated place for personal needs. We exited the cellar once the tornado passed and the storm was over. The storm caused tree limbs to break all over the front yard, and a bunch of little bantam chickens were running all over the place. Grandpa told us, "Whatever you do, please don't chase them because one of them crawls into a pop bottle for safety, and it's very difficult to get her out. So later that day, what do you think I did? I chased those little chickens until that one crawled into the bottle. Grandpa was outside cleaning up the yard with James, the oldest of the boys, and I'm sure he knew it was just a matter of time before the inevitable happened, and when it did, Grandpa approached me and said," What did I ask you not to do"?

I said, "Don't chase the chickens."

"Then he said, "I told you what would happen, didn't I?"

I said, "Yes." "How are you going to get her out?"

Grandpa told me, 'She knows how to get out, so leave the bottle there and sit on the porch and watch what she does." Sure enough, she was out and running around again in just a few seconds. I felt so much better.

And then there was Bell; she was Muskogee's pet cow, and she knew it! No one knew who Bell belonged to, but you would hear the cowbell around her neck every morning as she passed by Grandpa's farm. We would hear the ringing every evening around the same time, letting us know she was on her way home. In the evenings, my siblings and I would gather around Bell, pet her, and give her some water and straw, and then she would continue.

One day Daddy told my sister Johnnie to teach me how to tie my shoes because I would start attending school in September. Every evening just before dinner, we would sit on the couch and practice, but I wanted to watch tv instead, which upset Johnnie. So, Grandpa would come and sit with me while my sister went to eat dinner with the others because I wouldn't cooperate. They had chili dogs, french fries, and fresh homemade crackling, but I ate a peanut butter and jelly sandwich and a glass of milk and went to bed.

Most of the time, the four older siblings would leave in the morning and attend summer school. At the same time, Anitra, Leonard, and I would hang out with Grandpa and Mama and visit other relatives; in the evenings, we would sit on the porch, watch the fireflies, and listen to the crickets and June bugs. One evening while trying to catch fireflies, I saw something that looked like a hand coming out of a hole in the ground. It scared me, and I screamed so loud that everyone heard me. Grandpa came over and told me that's just a tarantula, and then he picked it up, let us pet it, and then put it back in front of its hole.

On our way into the house, I noticed that Grandfather took another path to what seemed to be a small garden, and he would stay over there for about another half hour before coming inside. When he came inside, I asked him, Grandpa, what was over there? And he told me he would show me tomorrow. The next day would be the last day of our visit with Grandpa, so many of our relatives came by to spend time with us; it was a very busy and fun day. After everyone left, Grandpa and I went over to the small garden, where he began to show and tell me about all the flowers and vegetables growing there and how he would gather important information about how each could benefit health and medicinal purposes. He even showed me an orange watermelon that he grew after cross–breeding a red and yellow. After a while, I noticed something darting around from flower to flower, and I asked him what it was. He said, "Those are Hummingbirds, "we stood watching them for a few more minutes until

Mama called for us to come for dinner. I'm grateful for this pleasant love-share moment with my Grandpa James Maddox.

Peace

Peace is a special Gift for all from the All for a Pleasant Life of Love.

Peace gives one a pleasant and powerful sense of Being.

Peace gives one a more profound sense of self.

Peace gives one a Brighter sense of what Life is about.

Peace gives one a more open mind, spirit, soul and body to receive the All's message.

Peace gives one a much greater sense of who the All is.

Peace gives one a much deeper sense of pleasantness in their life experience.

Peace gives one a much brighter sense of Hope for all.

Peace gives one a more pleasant sense of Peace with greater Love.

Peace of mind, spirit, soul and body makes one wiser.

Peace of mind, spirit, soul and body gives one more wisdom and wellness.

Peace of mind, spirit, soul and body allows one to receive clearly the message from the All creator of all.

Peace of mind, spirit, soul and body empowers one to communicate without words.

Peace of mind, spirit, soul and body allows us to Live Love and keep Pleasant Order.

Peace of mind, spirit, soul and body helps those in positions of authority to justly fairly regulate earthly affairs.

Peace of mind, spirit, soul and body will allow one to create a pleasant and peaceful working and living environments for all.

Peace of mind spirit soul and body allows one to harmonize with nature creating a very pleasant melody for all to experience.

Life
Experience

It was around six in the morning, and everyone was still asleep, but I wasn't feeling too well and needed to go to the bathroom badly. At this point, I didn't think much about how serious this was, so I slowly went to the bathroom; this is when things began to change for the worse. As I sat on the toilet, I started feeling very dizzy and faint, and when I got up, my equilibrium was pretty much off, making it difficult for me to walk; I began to worry. By the time I reached the door, I was sweating profusely, and after taking my first step out of the bathroom, I went down face first, landing on a bag of clothes outside my daughter Lydia's bedroom door. I thought I would transition until I saw what I believe were ancestral beings of light come toward me. It must have been at least four; I'm not sure how long I was down there, but after regaining consciousness, I felt a sense of pleasant peace and realized that this life experience took place for me to understand that I have a Life Purpose to fulfill. Like they say in the church,

God is not through with me yet! I was given a prayer that goes like this—Father God, please greatly gift me with greater-pleasant peace of mind, spirit, soul, and body so that I may love-share this life experience with those who choose to read this gift you have gifted me through, *"EIGHT STRANDS OF GOLD."*

Life

Life is what allows all things to dwell in love.

Life is what we all enjoy and share with each other.

Life makes us feel alive and this gives us peace.

Life should always be cherished for without it we are not.

Life must never be misused for it only comes once.

Life must never be taken for granted but always cherished for the gift that it is.

Life is a gift to all from the All.

Life must never be forgotten for it will never forget you.

Life must always be living for if not so too all things will be not living.

Life is the essence of all living things because it never stops giving.

Life will always preserve, protect, produce and provide.

Life will never stop for it is All.

Life must never stop for if it does so too will all things.

Life gives life to all things expecting nothing in return.

Life will always provide all things with sun and rain, the elements of life preservation.

Life can never be stopped by the works of humans.

Life will never allow anyone to cause death to Mother Earth.

Life awakens all things by gifting them with Love.

Life will never stop loving all for when it does it no longer loves itself.

Life will never stop for it is the essence of love.

Life must always share itself with all other beings for without Life none of them would exist.

Life is the Greatest Gift of Love.

Life is not only the greatest gift of love but also the most powerful gift from the All.

LIFE WILL ALWAYS BE.

Life is the essence of Love and Love the essence of Life one without the other is NOTHING.

Life
Experience

My observation tells me that humans still have much to learn about life.

This question arises often, and I'm sure not only in my mind but many others—Why are we still so quick to destroy ourselves and the beings of so many other species? Why do so few take so much, leaving so many with so little?

Life is a Gift from the All, the one who truly gives love, life, and wellness to our mind, spirit, soul, and body. Life must never be considered something we deserve because we are a specific race, creed, or color. It must be honored for its contribution to humanity. Life is not just waking up and going to school or work; it is an experience with a specific purpose for each person. How many life purposes have been destroyed due to war? In other words, think about the number of children who never truly had the opportunity to experience life and, even more importantly, how many would have chosen to teach their children that all men are created equal.

There is a Law of Order for the Preservation of Life seen in all creation— the four elements air, water, earth, fire, and aquatic life. They also include creatures of the planet, such as the fowl of the air, the four seasons, the ebb and flow of the ocean's tide, the rise and set of the sun, the rotation of the earth, and orbiting of other planets. We can learn much from life by simply observing creation.

In summary, life is not what most of us think it is, it is not a duration of time, measured from birth to death, but life is infinite; life is God! When you and I transition from this realm of life, life will continue as it always has for an unprecedented number of generations. Love is the essence of life and the essence of love; both are a Gift from All!

Made in the USA
Columbia, SC
08 May 2024

35048796R00043